Simplicity

MADE EASY

Simplicity
MADE EASY

Jennifer Kavanagh

BOOKS

Winchester, UK
Washington, USA

First published by O-Books, 2011
O-Books is an imprint of John Hunt Publishing Ltd., Laurel House, Station Approach,
Alresford, Hants, SO24 9JH, UK
office1@o-books.net
www.o-books.com

For distributor details and how to order please visit the 'Ordering' section on our website.

Text copyright: Jennifer Kavanagh 2010

ISBN: 978 1 84694 543 4

A CIP catalogue record for this book is available from the British Library.

Design: Stuart Davies

Printed in the UK by CPI Antony Rowe
Printed in the USA by Offset Paperback Mfrs, Inc

We operate a distinctive and ethical publishing philosophy in all
areas of our business, from our global network of authors to
production and worldwide distribution.

CONTENTS

by the same author
The Methuen Book of Animal Tales (ed.)
The Methuen Book of Humorous Stories (ed.)
Call of the Bell Bird
The World is our Cloister
New Light (ed.)
The O of Home

'Tis the gift to be simple, 'tis the gift to be free,
'Tis the gift to come down where we ought to be,
And when we find ourselves in the place just right,
'Twill be in the valley of love and delight.
When true simplicity is gain'd,
To bow and to bend we shan't be asham'd,
To turn, turn will be our delight,
Till by turning, turning we come round right.
Nineteenth-century Shaker song

Preface

Simplicity is neither simple to achieve nor easy to define.

Is it the opposite of complexity? Is it a lack of elaboration or a lack of excess? It may be all these things, but there is a positive quality to simplicity that is more than a set of negatives, and surpasses form. But how does any of this apply to us? What is a simple life, and why should we want to lead one?

Traditionally, simplicity has been associated with our attitude to material possessions. Figures as diverse as Jesus, Gandhi, Confucius, Marcus Aurelius and the Buddha considered a preoccupation with the material world to be a barrier to the spiritual life. Our own motivation to simplify our life may come from a concern to leave a smaller carbon footprint or a wish simply to downsize. It may relate to material objects or excessive busyness; it may be expressed in ridding ourselves of possessions or becoming less attached, but it is likely that the motivation to live a simpler life will spring from an inner compulsion.

Simplicity is not just a lifestyle option, but an attitude of mind, a path for the inner as well as the outer life. It is not a narrowing of life, but a distillation. It is not so much to do with possessions, as with our attitude to them. After all "the root of all evil", it is said, is not money but *the love of* money". Simplicity, as Duane Elgin says, is "not self-denying but life-affirming" (167). It is also not just about ourselves. A simple life will encompass not only our own needs, but those of others, and those of the environment in which we live.

What we will seek to do in this book is to unpick the different approaches to simplicity and consider some of the steps, as well as some of the dangers, on the way. For simplicity is not a goal to be achieved, but a lifelong process.

To begin with, let us be clear that we are talking about a

conscious choice, a deliberate act. There is nothing glorious about enforced poverty. Elgin makes the point that we are not talking either about some reversion to a childlike or primitive state. We are adults living in a complex world, and it is with our adult understanding and knowledge of the modern world that we need to find a way that integrates our creativity and our sense of moral purpose. On the other hand, as we will see in Chapter 9, history, folklore and the stories from many faiths show us that sometimes it takes the clear sight of a child, or a clown, to cut through the pretence of modern life.

Chapter I

Background

In folk history and philosophy, in the arts and in science, simplicity has generally been considered "a good thing". People from such different cultures and periods of history as Confucius, Lao-Tzu, Thoreau and Gandhi have paid tribute to its importance. The German writer, Goethe, wrote: "Nothing is true, but that which is simple." John Ruskin felt that "it is far more difficult to be simple than to be complicated; far more difficult to sacrifice skill and easy execution in the proper place, than to expand both indiscriminately." A principle established by William of Ockham, a fourteenth-century Franciscan friar and philosopher, states that "entities must not be multiplied beyond necessity". In other words, the simplest explanation or strategy tends to be the best one. Stripped of all excess or unnecessary matter, the truth, the essence, shines through. Undue elaboration, complication or, indeed, obfuscation, masks the message, the purpose, of almost everything. It is certainly a barrier to communication. We all know examples of the jargon used by particular professions to exclude, as it seems to us, anyone not in the know. When it is a matter of information given out by government, it is vital that it is comprehensible to the general public. For over thirty years, the Plain English campaign has been working to eradicate gobbledygook and jargon from our public information, so that we can indeed be informed. Simple, spare prose is effective. As Ruskin said, "The greatest thing a human soul ever does in this world is to see something, and to tell what it saw in a plain way."

Simple elegance and clear lines are admired in most aspects of design – whether of clothes, architecture or furniture. The culture of the Shakers, a religious group founded in the eighteenth century, is particularly renowned for the way functionality, simplicity and beauty are combined, the way "form follows function". Shakers never fashioned items with elaborate details or extra decorations, but only made things for their intended uses. The interior spaces of their buildings are characterised by austerity and simplicity, and the simple architecture of their homes, meeting houses, and barns have had a lasting influence on American architecture and design. But it is for their simple, functional and high quality furniture that the Shakers are best known, and still emulated.

Worship

Shakers came out of a religious revolution that began in seventeenth-century England: simplicity was an aspect of their faith. Part of the general Protestant movement, in fact, was to simplify worship itself. It was felt that to remove what were seen as the "Popish" trappings of High church services – incense, rich vestments, etc. – would enable worshippers to focus on what mattered: the worship of the Divine. Quakers, for instance, stripped away the rituals and externals of religious services; their practice to this day is utterly simple in its lack of set words, dogma, anything that might interfere with the relationship between the worshippers and God. Quaker Meetings for Worship can take place at any time and in any place – no building is more sacred than another – and Meeting Houses themselves are bare of symbols and ornamentation. Quakers feel that cumbersome theology can be simplified into the statement "God is love". One wrote recently: "The more overlaid our reaching out to that ultimate reality is with ritual, words, music and image, the more it is masked by human reality" (Quaker Quest, 21).

In reform Islam too there has been a stripping down of the accretions of ritual and superstition accrued over the centuries. In the eighteenth century, the Arabian scholar, Abdul Wahhab, became aware of the luxury in dress and behaviour, what he considered as superstitious pilgrimages to shrines, the use of omens and the worship given to Muhammad and Muslim saints rather than to God. He began a mission to purify the religion, to proclaim the simplicity of the early religion founded on the Koran and the manner of life of Muhammad.

Meditation, at the centre of many Eastern religions, requires practitioners to leave behind all distractions, everything save the experience of the present moment. Focus and concentration are at its heart. An image or a prayer is chosen as a focus; attention to this is sustained and repeated on a regular basis. Insight meditation is an all-encompassing practice, a way to healing, purification, detachment and awareness by concentrating on different parts of the body, or pain of the mind or heart. Practice is built up over a long period; steadfastness and concentration are the keynotes. What is required is a willingness to let go of everything and go to the centre of our being.

Zen Buddhism goes further, letting go even of the need for a focus for meditation. With inner experience at its heart, stripped of both dogma and the authority of sacred books, Zen is neither a religion nor a philosophy: its fundamental objective is to obtain insight into the nature of our mind and soul. It eschews intellectual analysis and religious doctrine, trying to grasp the central fact of life as it is lived. "Zen teaches nothing," writes D.T. Suzuki, one of the foremost authorities on Zen. "We teach ourselves; Zen merely points the way" (38). Elusive to all but the most experienced practitioner, Zen can be seen as the epitome of simplicity.

Regardless of label, there can be no simpler practice than sitting down and opening up the self to the Divine, or Higher Being.

A simple life
But what does simplicity mean when it is applied to our own

daily lives? We live in a complex world, and it is not surprising if we sometimes feel it is all just too much. Assailed on every side by information, weaving our way through life's options can be an exhausting and puzzling business.

Albert Einstein is quoted as saying, "When the solution is simple, God is answering", and in a religious context, "simplicity" takes on a particular significance. When we apply simplicity to our own lives, when we strip away the unnecessary, the extraneous from ourselves, we become more truly who we are, and as such we reveal the potential we were born to express. A favourite definition of simplicity for me is to remove the clutter between ourselves and God, or the Spirit, or the real self – whichever expression we find comfortable.

What that clutter is will be different for each one of us. Traditionally, much of the extraneous matter, the clutter that obscures the essence, has been seen as material wealth. Buddha relinquished his wealth and embraced a life of noble poverty; in Jesus' life, the shedding of material possessions was a prominent theme. We will look at the subject of "stuff" in Chapter 3.

Over the centuries, many religious followers have taken a lack of material wealth as an end in itself, have missed the possibility that shedding possessions might be a means to an end. But what is this end? What is the point of simplicity? If in simplifying our lives we are stripping away the inessentials, then the real questions are: What is left? What is the purpose of my life? By the very process of removing the clutter, the answer will become clearer.

What we "clutter" our lives with can take many forms, and we will consider some of them in the following chapters.

Chapter 2

Beginnings

Begin where you are
Thomas Kelly (60)

So you'd like to simplify your life? Perhaps it feels heavy and chaotic. The demands of possessions and countless activities get in the way. It's hard to see the wood for the trees; you feel you are running to stand still. You'd like to have a clearer purpose, be less distracted, have a life less trammelled with irrelevancies or excess, more time for what really matters. How to begin?

A way of life is rarely static. From an early age, social pressures are likely to move us in the direction of building a lifestyle to reflect increasing success and affluence. We expect to buy more, acquire bigger, better and more fashionable houses, furniture and clothes. At a certain point in our lives, maybe when children have grown up, or when financial burdens oppress us, we may wish to downsize, to live more lightly. Moving to a simpler way of life may seem a good idea, but while it remains at the level of thought, it is unlikely to take root as a practical possibility. It is only when there is a gut instinct, a sense of heart-felt momentum, that we are likely to take action.

Change usually comes as a result of a growing awareness and will often be felt as discomfort: a niggling unease that is hard to define. We just know that something is not right. Reaching a place of clarity can be painfully slow. Jonathan Dale writes well about the "nagging" process:

> Of course it wasn't my family that was nagging me, nor my friends...It was something else. It was quietly there again and

again and again – part of the very fabric of our lives. It never let me go. It wasn't threatening. It wasn't paralysing. It wasn't a command. It was an inner conversation which always ended with my being shown how my lifestyle was inconsistent with my professed beliefs. It was infinitely patient and quietly persuasive. It was the Light in spoken form and it nagged me lovingly into something which I knew in my heart of hearts that I wanted to do, however long my resistance (75-6).

There is a story about William Penn, founder of the state of Pennsylvania. Part of his apparel as an aristocrat was to wear a sword. He asked George Fox, one of the early members of the Religious Society of Friends (Quakers), whether it was all right to wear one. Fox's response was not "Take it off this instant; we are a pacifist organisation" but "Wear it as long as you can." I find that a good rule to live by: eat meat for as long as you can, fly to overseas holidays for as long as you can, drink alcohol for as long as you can; give up when and if the discomfort grows too much. Pay attention to the inner truth. We speak of having choices and, of course, compared to those who struggle to survive, we do. But to talk of making decisions is to speak from an external perspective. There is an interior imperative, and the way becomes clear.

Change is not a once-and-for-all event but a gradual process. As we make changes, so we will feel moved to make others. Jonathan Dale talks of "going beyond the comfort zone" in the wrestling with our daily choices in travel, housing and shopping. And wrestling it is. "How far is enough? Should we feel virtuous for being a vegetarian or guilty for not being a vegan? Is it good to trade in a BMW for a mini, or should we be cycling to the station? Such questions arise continuously, yet there can be no straightforward answer" (quoted in Dale, 23). I know that when I was working in a poor Bangladeshi community in the East End of London I felt a discomfort in returning to my own comfortable flat. It is in listening to that discomfort that we make changes in our lives.

The motivation for change will be personal: we may feel moved by the effects of climate change, by a wish to free ourselves from the weight of our possessions, or by compassion for those who have so much less. Whatever the motivation, to attach a moral dimension to simplicity is to misunderstand. There are no shoulds and oughts in this journey; guilt about possessions, competitiveness about how little, as well as how much, we own, are dangerous and missing the point. Taking pleasure in self-denial is just another aspect of pride.

Nor is change likely to be the result of external demands. We are unlikely to change our lives because we are told to, and if we do, if the move has not come from our own clarity, it is unlikely to be sustainable. Without taking ownership, our response is likely to be backward-looking and resentful. We may have shed material possessions, but an inner simplicity will not be the result.

As people move towards simplicity, for reasons of sustainability, solidarity, or simple practicality, they will have followed an inner imperative that will not, in the end, be denied. As with other movements of the spirit, simplicity can be both a cause and an effect. As a spiritual path develops, so there is a yearning for a simpler life; as we simplify our life, so the inner voice becomes clearer, and we find a need for more quiet time alone to tune in.

Chapter 3

Stuff and spareness

My life was blessed in that I never needed anything until I had it.
Hassidic rabbi

Shopping has become an addiction in Western society. It's become a hugely popular leisure activity for its own sake, rather than a response to a need. So much is on offer that spontaneous selection is high. The more we visit shops, the more tempted we are to buy things beyond our original intentions. In the early days of our marriage, when we had very little money, my husband and I went to the supermarket just once a month, so that we would be less frequently tempted to buy more than we actually needed, planned, or could afford.

Much of what we have we don't even want. Bargains that we bought in the sales, but never much liked once we got them home, clothes that we are hoping will come back into fashion, or that we are waiting to shrink back into. Books that we have read and know we will not re-read, or that we intended to read, but are never likely to open. Junk mail, old newspapers, out-of-date catalogues and correspondence. There may come a time when we are aware that we have too much stuff! The feeling might come from a need to move into a smaller flat or house, or because the pressure of belongings has become stifling. We are aware of duplication, things we don't use, presents given us that we have never really liked. We feel disloyal if we give away something given to us in love or friendship, worry that the donor will notice its absence when they visit. But if it is neither useful nor beautiful, why do we allow it to clutter up our life?

Maybe, in the same spirit as the old habit of spring cleaning, we should take time once a year to go through our clothes, books and old papers, and some of our routine habits. Do we need to take a daily paper now that we hear much of the news on radio or TV? Do we need to keep up, for instance, a life insurance now that we have no dependants? In the UK the Royal Mail runs an opt-out service for unaddressed mail sent to a particular address; Direct Marketing covers a lot of other organisations that send out unsolicited mail. Taking the trouble to contact them will deal with irritation in the future, and maybe save a few trees. However boring the process, however hard the choices, once begun, there is a sense of freedom and space that makes continuing a positive act.

But what do we do when people keep giving us things? If we feel we don't need to acquire anything else, we can encourage friends to give a goat or a tree on our behalf to someone in need, through one of the many charities that offer that service. Many couples marrying for a second time or later in life when they have all that they need simply don't want to be given anything else, and ask for donations to be given to charity. I know a couple who instead of wedding gifts asked for money to pay for national insurance for a whole village in Ghana. If presents still come our way, a policy of one in, one out can be an option. If I buy or am given, for instance, a book, I try to give one away. Otherwise, the shelves (and I) will once again begin to groan! Not a hard and fast rule, perhaps, but a general tendency.

It is not only quantity of belongings that might trouble us, but a sense of disorder: things begun and not finished, loose ends that get in the way of what we really want to do. Again, there might be some tough decisions, but the ability to discard what no longer has purpose, and to pick up the pieces of what does matter to us, will give us renewed energy and sense of direction. Listening to our inner voice will clarify what is truly important. I was given fresh insight, for instance, by a friend's recent comment that the opposite of simplicity is not complexity but chaos.

For practitioners of the ancient Chinese system of aesthetics, *feng shui*, physical clutter is a serious problem. At the heart of the practice is arranging living spaces in such a way as to create a positive flow of energy, so clutter is seen as literally blocking the energy flow. Practitioners consider clutter as damaging to our health, making us tired and depressed. In a cluttered room, our energy stagnates, our mood declines, and our focus dwindles. There's no energy to bring in new ideas and inspiration. (www.onsimplicity.net)

Much to my surprise, I have felt moved to give away much of what I owned. After a year of travel it became clear that I had no need of most of what I had left behind. The trappings of that middle-class life no longer represented the me I had become. In giving away or selling furniture, books and other belongings, I felt a joyous sense of freedom and lightness. There was less to be responsible for, to insure, take care of, to dust! And the process continues.

Exceptionally, a friend was clear from an early age that he had only to trust, and his needs would be met:

> I felt that I should only take from life what I needed to sustain myself and to give back whatever I could. I also felt that by living from my love outwards, which meant giving all I could in my work, I would always have enough to get by.
> Quaker Quest, 29

If we are privileged to spend time in countries where the standard of living is much below our own, where a job is a rarity, where much of the day is spent in fetching water and making a fire to cook on, and where basic necessities are hard to come by, it is easier to understand how spoilt we are; how much more we have than we need, and how, even with so little, their lives can be richer than ours. Experiencing the contrast can be life-changing, but we need to be careful. The example of others with little choice may be humbling and influential, but we must not forget that our own movement towards living with less has been freely chosen; theirs has not.

As mentioned in the first chapter, most religions consider that absorption in material possessions is a barrier to a spiritual life. Jesus was clear:

> If thou wilt be perfect, go and sell that thou hast, and give to the poor, and thou shalt have treasure in heaven: and come and follow me…Verily I say unto you, That a rich man shall hardly enter into the kingdom of heaven.
>
> And again I say unto you, It is easier for a camel to go through the eye of a needle, than for a rich man to enter into the kingdom of God.
> Matthew 19:21-24 AV

And in Mark

> Go thy way, sell whatsoever thou hast, and give to the poor, and thou shalt have treasure in heaven: and come, take up the cross, and follow me…
>
> How hardly shall they that have riches enter into the kingdom of God!
> Mark 10:21-23 AV

The Christian monastic tradition requires renunciation and detachment, demanding that monks divest themselves of all money and personal possessions, relying instead on communal resources. In general, that is not to go without; the community looks after its own, and in old age community members are cared for, and a burial paid for. Maybe we can learn from the monastic example of sharing. How much do we actually need to own? Books can be borrowed from libraries; perhaps our local council has started up a car pool for shared use. Do we need to own a property?

Nearer to "real" poverty is the life of the Indian mendicant or *sannyasi*, who in old age leaves home and possessions behind and travels with a begging bowl, committing himself to a life of insecurity and dependence on others for alms.

But what is the point of this kind of self-denial? Although it is unlikely that many of us will be called to such an extreme response, it is true that the more attention we pay to our possessions, the less we have for our inner life. Quite simply, an excess of things gets in the way. Things have a tendency to take us over: time and money are needed for their upkeep. The more possessions we have, the more attention needs to be paid to their maintenance. Consider how much it costs in time and money to keep up a big house: roof, woodwork, decoration, not to mention the heating. Think about how much time we spend in deciding what to wear: to choose from the array of clothes in our cupboards and wardrobes. What will look good? What is right for this occasion? Does my bum look big in this? Spending attention on externals. With less to look after, we have more time and attention to apply to our inner life and the needs of others.

In any case, spareness in daily life is a pleasure in itself. A vehicle for mindfulness, it concentrates the mind on the present moment and on what there is. In a basement flat, a patch of blue sky is precious; in the desert the tracery of the trail of a single black beetle captures the heart; a single flower in an urban window box can be more treasured than the lushness of a country garden. Quality supersedes quantity. There is an intensity of experience that is a welcome counter to the usual hurried and superficial quality of our attention.

Nor is it just the ownership and presence of material objects that gets in the way, but the constant distraction that they represent. Our attachment to our belongings is very often for sentimental reasons: each is a reminder of someone we love or something in our past. For many, such reminders are precious. In each life, it will become clear whether the priority is to keep or let go of particular possessions. We may find that we do not need objects to remind us of people we love; that we no longer want souvenirs to draw us into another time, away from an immediate focus. We may wish to be present, both in time and in space.

Non-attachment

Asceticism is not that you should not own anything, but that nothing should own you.
Ali Ibn Abi Talib (ca. 596-661)

We are the things we possess, we are that to which we are attached.
Krishnamurti

Our attitude to material possessions is often more important than how much we actually own. A preoccupation with how much we own can absorb as much of our attention as the objects themselves. The ecumenical Christian Iona community has developed a model of economic simplicity, with an emphasis on equality and detachment:

We follow an economic model which is based on need. Everyone receives an allowance which is the same regardless of job, qualifications, professional standing, age or experience... This poverty is not one of hardship. Rather it is one of simplicity, and of corporate responsibility for money...sharing limited space and material resources...sharing responsibility for appropriate budgeting, all tend towards detachment from material possessions and towards an appreciation of those things that cannot be bought with money.

Members living away from the island give a tenth of their income to the community (for charity and the common fund) and engage in open discussion about their use of the other ninety per cent.

There is a Jewish story about a man trying to find a spiritual master. In the town he finds a teacher living in a fine house, surrounded by possessions, and he turns away in disgust. In the desert he finds a man in rags sitting on a rock.

> "Just imagine," he said, "the first teacher I went to was surrounded with possessions."
>
> The man on the rock began to cry.
>
> "Why are you crying?" the seeker asked in astonishment.
>
> "That teacher has possessions because he is detached from them; I couldn't handle them, which is why I am here."

Attachment often stems from a need for security. Money and possessions can assume the role of a comfort blanket: surrounding ourselves with familiar objects can enlarge our sense of self and insulate us from the realities of a sometimes challenging world. I don't think we can make ourselves be less attached: it's part of a bigger journey in which the importance of non-material things looms larger in our lives, and we wish to give them space. What we can do is work towards recognition of what is and is not important, and then act on it.

Non-attachment is a concept central to many Eastern religions, a concept that goes way beyond an attitude to material possessions. This brings us to a deeper level of simplicity, which will be explored in Chapter 10.

Chapter 4

Time and busyness

This day will not come again
Nyogen Senzaki, trans. Paul Reps

An aspect of simplicity that is often ignored is the use of time, something that in the hurly burly of modern life appears to be in short supply. In lives of work, family, leisure activities – just the upkeep of our possessions, and the paperwork that increases by the year – we feel rushed, harried, with no time to call our own. And the higher our material standard of living is, the more we need to work to keep it up.

It is not just that we fill up all the available time, that we work hard and for long hours, but what we fill it with is so fragmented; our attention is pulled in so many directions. When we are asked what we have done today, we remember one or two central activities, but forget the hundreds of smaller tasks and preoccupations: washing, filling up the car, filling in our tax return, paying the electricity bill, thinking about what to cook, what to wear, what to buy. Modern life is so complicated, and we complicate it further in our pride in multi-tasking. Above all, and especially in our work lives, we are fixated on results, on productivity, efficiency – as if we were machines. Who are we in all of this? In our endless doing, where is our being?

We seem addicted to speed. Even when we do not need to, we rush to complete a task in order to get on with the next one. What are we hurrying to? Even reading a book that I'm enjoying, I find myself flicking through the pages to see how much more there is to read. Why? Why not stay on the page, in the moment, and enjoy it?

At the end of the day, it is no wonder that we need a drink to help us relax, that we have energy for nothing except to slump in front of the television and then fall into bed. And, the next day, we have to start all over again. In squeezing in more and more activities, we have too little time to give to our relationships, to what really matters in our lives. There is no time, as Cecil Collins puts it, for "the leisure of the soul"; "no leisure to form a communion with life itself" (3). The common cry of the workaholic spouse that "I'm doing it for you!" undervalues the needs of the family for the precious gift of attention.

Many people find that at a certain point in their lives, in mid-life perhaps, or after a serious illness or traumatic personal event, they want to review their lives, their commitments, their jobs. The niggle of dissatisfaction that has burrowed its way into their consciousness finally will not be denied. Life feels too short to be constantly under stress, working late, bringing work home. Maybe they begin to reassess the importance of productivity and efficiency, and to question the meaning of "success". Some decide to make radical changes in their lives, to give up the demands of a stressful job to do something that maybe takes up less time, maybe is more personally rewarding, even if the impact of such a shift means a reduced income and a less lavish lifestyle.

Even within our current working lives, somehow we have to find a way to free ourselves of constant preoccupation, to clear a space in our minds and hearts, as well as in our living rooms. That applies to all purposeful activity, whether in the home or at work; voluntary action, as well as money-making activities. In a working life and within the family, creative ways may have to be found to give ourselves that space. Maybe we can reduce the time given to our social lives, have fewer house guests, make mental space a priority, learn to say "no". Maybe we might stop watching so much news, reduce the amount of information that fills our brains at the expense of reflection and contemplation.

Allow time to collect ourselves, pay attention, be mindful. There has to be time to be still, to allow our consciousness to expand beyond the distractions of the everyday, the pressing of clock-related activities, time for timelessness to take over, for intuition to let its voice be heard. We need to distance ourselves from the "and then, and then" of our hectic lives, the plans of an ego-driven life, the racing mind so hard to dissolve in meditation, to give attention to the stillness of the heart.

> Paradoxical as it may seem, the purposeful life has no content, no point. It hurries on and on, and misses everything. Not hurrying, the purposeless life misses nothing, for it is only when there is no goal and no rush that the human senses are fully open to receive the world. Absence of hurry also involves a certain lack of interference with the natural course of events, especially when it is felt that the natural course follows principles which are not foreign to human intelligence. For…the Taoist mentality makes, or forces, nothing but "grows" everything.
> Watts, 195

When I can, I take my watch off to take "time" out of the equation, let the natural instincts of hunger, awareness of dawn and dusk, take precedence. In Native American cultures the passage of time is viewed as not linear but circular, part of the cyclic nature of the seasons, the rising and setting of the sun, the birth, growth, maturing and death of all creation: plants, animals and people. Being in touch with that motion of time is to be part of the interconnectedness of all creation.

Even in terms of our own efficiency, taking time "out" can pay dividends. The "Eureka" moment came for Archimedes not when he was concentrating hard, but when he had let go of his preoccupations. It was when he stepped into the bath that inspiration came. We may all be familiar with solutions coming to us after "sleeping on" a problem; growth often takes place once the soil has lain fallow.

Noise

Noise too can be a barrier to a more authentic life. We learn, after all, that the Spirit is heard in "a still small voice". It is hard to hear or feel God, the Spirit, or our inner voice if there is competition for our attention. A background of noise is a commonplace in public places – muzak in shops; frequent announcements on public transport – and it is even more so in our private spaces. Frequent unsolicited phonecalls from marketing services ("junk noise") can disrupt the peace of our leisure time. Sometimes the frequency is such that people have been driven to stop answering their phones. In the UK a call to the Telephone Preference Service can stop a good number of these calls.

But most of the noise that surrounds us at home is of our own choosing. A background of radio or our favourite music is a constant accompaniment to many lives; the MP3 player comes with us on journeys to work, even jogging in the park or on the beach. Ownership of an iPhone means we are continuously "in touch" with the outside world. The inside world doesn't have a chance. We are scared, it seems, of the void.

Not surprisingly, silence is an important component of the spiritual practice of most religions. It's hard to find in the modern world, and maybe it's more realistic – and more appropriate – to talk of "stillness", which is something we can work towards. In meditation and silent worship it is hard to stop the chatter of our busy "monkey" brains, but only in inner stillness do we stand any chance not only of tranquillity but of a moment of enlightenment. In stillness, the mind and heart turn inwards towards the spirit within; it is a place of listening. Finding a part of the day in which we hold ourselves in stillness, freeing ourselves as much as possible from external demands, can become an important part of our daily lives. Even in the midst of a busy working life, it is possible to pause, take moments of stillness, to centre or collect ourselves. It's a good discipline that can be carried out anywhere: waiting at a bus stop, sitting on the Tube, or waiting for a kettle to boil.

Mindfulness

A distinct pause before embarking on any activity makes its intentionality clear, and concentrates the mind on the shift of attention from one thing to another. Without such pauses, it is all too easy to live on an abstracted automatic pilot, torn by one responsibility after another, rushing from one action to another, without paying much attention to any of them. How much attention do we give to anything we do in that mindset? How much do we value it? Even when we stop, we are often abstracted, our minds preoccupied. We might gaze out of the window, but see nothing, looking *through* rather than *at*.

Being present, living "mindfully" is about living more consciously, with more awareness – more simply. Everything takes on a sharper definition; we are more aware of the detail of our surroundings, more sensitive to the needs of the people around us, the beauty of a leaf blowing outside the window. Instead of seeking stimulation from the new and the special, we may begin to recapture the importance of the familiar, the commonplace, the everyday, the "ordinary". Recently, in order to counter my natural instinct to eat too quickly, I have taken to eating with chopsticks occasionally to slow myself down. And, sometimes, I shut my eyes while eating. It is surprising how intensified the experience becomes: how strong the taste, how distinct the textures, of the food.

We are also pulled away from the present by attachment to the past or anxiety about the future, another aspect of our preoccupation with security. The past – whether recollected with nostalgia or regret – may not have been as we remember, and in any case it has gone. The future is not yet here, and we cannot foretell it. Anxiety about what might happen is a waste of time and energy, and, more importantly, an indication of a lack of trust. If we go forth in faith, anxiety will not be part of our lives. When something worries me, I find it useful to ask myself, "Will it matter in a year's time? Does it matter to people on the other side of the world?" The answer is almost invariably "no".

Mindfulness is the simple awareness of what one is doing while one is doing it, and of nothing else. The systematic practice of mindfulness, based on *satipatthana*, a discourse given by the Buddha, is central to all forms of Buddhism. The four "foundations" or areas of awareness are: of the body and senses, the heart and feelings, mind and thoughts, and awareness of the principles that govern life.

> Often in daily life, our body and mind may not be together. Sometimes our body is here but our mind is lost in the past or in the future. We may be possessed by anger, hatred, jealousy, or anxiety. If we practise the teaching of the Buddha on how to breathe mindfully, we bring mind and body together, and they become one again.
>
> Hanh, 53

The practice of mindfulness is extensive, not only in Buddhism. When I read recently, "Before changing action, pause and remember who you are", my first thought was that that means knowing who we are in the first place, and then I realised that "remember" can also be seen as the opposite of "dismember". "Recollection" and "self-remembering" are also expressions of bringing the self back to an awareness of the present moment.

In a God-centred faith, recollection will be to the Spirit within and to God's will. *The Practice of the Presence of God* is a slim volume of letters and conversations describing just that: a way of life in which everything is done for the glory of God: an active title for an active expression of our faith. Brother Lawrence, a seventeenth-century French lay brother, spent years washing up in the monastery kitchen, every moment consecrated, in the present and in the Presence. His was a life of the greatest simplicity.

.

Chapter 5

A compassionate life

Help is no virtue but an artery of existence
Martin Buber

Up to now we have dealt mostly with ways in which we, as
individuals, can simplify our lives. But living simply is not just
about individual choices: our lives need to be seen in the context
of the world in which we live, and the people we live among.
However small it feels, our contribution can help transform the
world into a more balanced and equal place.

Mostly, we take our wealth for granted – indeed, we might
sometimes feel that we are pretty hard up. Only when the
comparisons made are not with successful friends, neighbours
or celebrities, but with those who have so much less than we do,
do we understand our own good fortune. Only when faced with
pictures of starving children or maybe when we hear a first-
hand account of how it feels to be homeless, do we feel uncomfortable. Uncomfortable – and helpless. What can we do with
our discomfort? The poverty and inequality of the world feel too
big for us to cope with.

For some people, the gulf between their own wealth and the
poverty elsewhere will provide an incentive, or even a
compulsion, to strip away their own comfort and riches. They
will feel driven to live simply in order to live alongside the poor,
to put themselves on a level with those who have least, in a
spirit both of equality and the message of the Sermon on the
Mount. Fasting for part of the day as is the practice in many
Buddhist monasteries can be seen as part of a compassionate
solidarity with those in need.

Mother Teresa's Missionaries of Charity are commonly identified with the poorest and most marginalised in society, and move among them from a perspective in their own lives of the greatest simplicity. The Little Brothers of Jesus, founded by Charles de Foucault, also strive to live and work alongside the poor. One of their number, Charles Carretto, writes:

> If I love, if I really love, how can I tolerate the fact that a third of humanity is menaced by starvation while I enjoy the security of economic stability?...The Little Brother may not have a life apart. He must choose a village, a slum, a nomadic town and live as all the others live, especially as the poorest live.
>
> *Letters from the Desert*

Few of us feel called to make such an uncompromising response. Indeed, we may question its authenticity. If we feel unwilling or unable to make radical changes in our lives, but our discomfort tells us that what we are doing is not enough, a more modest approach might be to take a good look at our current life, and what we actually need. Can we be content with enough? Enough for our need but not our greed, as the saying goes. Each will answer according to his or her inner truth. Even small changes can have an impact on our own outlook, and be the beginning of something more.

Awareness of the needs of those less fortunate than ourselves is at the heart of most religions, and in many rules are laid down: Orthodox Jews are bidden to give ten per cent of their income to charity; for Muslims, it is considered to be a personal responsibility to ease economic hardship for others and eliminate inequality. *Zakāt* or alms-giving is obligatory for all who are able to do so. Sikh teachings also stress the concept of sharing through the distribution of free food at Sikh *gurdwaras*, giving charitable donations, and working for the good of the community and others.

Although the practice of tithing was prevalent in mediaeval England – farmers had to offer a tenth of their harvest, while craftsmen had to offer a tenth of their production – such donations were for the church or, later, the State, not directly for those in need. However, love for others, helping those who have least, is of course at the heart of Jesus' teachings.

The Vietnamese Buddhist Thich Nhat Hanh is quoted as saying: "Do not accumulate wealth while millions are hungry...Live simply and share time, energy, and material resources with those who are in need." As we make changes in our life, we become aware of the connections with our fellow human beings, and also with the rest of the creation.

A light footprint

Everything is connected; every choice we make – what we wear, what we eat – impacts on others. The use of disposable goods, and the quantity and disposal of our waste, together with recent publicity about climate change, have brought about an increased awareness of the impact of the Western way of life. Consideration of different kinds of fuel, concern about food miles and the use of air travel are no longer the preoccupation of a fringe group, but increasingly part of the political agenda. The additional pressure of recession in many countries has driven people to review the way in which they live.

Although our prime motivation for change may be our personal circumstances, we can no longer ignore the impact of our way of life on other people, and on the planet itself. Our interconnectedness with the rest of humanity, and with other created beings – which has been acknowledged by indigenous peoples for centuries – is at last more apparent to those of us in wealthier societies. Developing simplicity in our daily life can be an expression of that interconnectedness.

Food

We live in an age when almost any foodstuff is available at any time of year – if we have enough money to pay for it. Eating fresh fruit and vegetables in their natural season does not only reduce the cost of transport and forced growing conditions, but brings us back into connection with the cycles of the year. The limited availability of a vegetable during the winter enhances the delight we take in it as it comes into season. A harvest festival begins to recover some meaning.

Many people, particularly as they get older, are eating less meat and, after a number of health scares, are taking more care about the provenance of the meat they do eat. Others feel moved to give up meat altogether, and maybe fish; some become vegans, giving up dairy products too. A few, preferring not to kill anything, will become fruitarians, eating neither animal products nor vegetables nor grains. Some, wishing to avoid the energy consumption of cooking and the possible negative impact on the food of cooking it, prefer only to eat raw and unprocessed food. A balanced diet, which contains all the nutrients necessary for a healthy life, is difficult to obtain from a severely restricted diet, but millions of vegetarians and vegans all over the world live healthy lives.

Individual reasons for a change of diet might range from a wish not to eat dead animals to concern for the treatment of animals to more general concerns about the environment. Producing animal-based food, it seems, is less efficient in its use of land and water than the direct harvesting of grains, vegetables, seeds and fruit for human consumption. There is also evidence that "modern practices of raising animals for food contributes [sic]...to deforestation, air and water pollution, land degradation, loss of topsoil, climate change, the overuse of resources including oil and water, and loss of biodiversity." (See Wikipedia on environmental vegetarianism.)

We have come a long way since the domination of humans

over the animal kingdom was generally accepted. There is now more general concern about the welfare of animals: both the conditions in which they are kept and killed and their use for experimentation. More of us eat free range eggs and chickens, and we are beginning to take some care to avoid endangered varieties of fish.

But our consumption doesn't end with food. There are choices to be made about avoiding the use of endangered hardwoods in our furniture, about using carpets that have not been made in exploitative conditions. And clothes. Interest in ethical fashion is growing; more designers are interested in using organic materials and ethical production methods. Increasingly, attention is being paid to the provenance of our clothing, the "journey" of a garment. What happened with food is now happening with the clothes that we wear.

Change

Poverty, justice and climate change are huge concepts, and it is easy to feel that it is beyond our capacity to make a difference. But changes in our daily lives can be made in small steps. These are some of the steps that we might consider:

- buying fair trade
- using alternative sources of energy
- insulating our houses and flats
- lowering levels of personal consumption
- wearing more clothes indoors and turning the heating down
- using products that are non-polluting, durable and easy to repair
- living without a car, or cutting down on its use
- trying not to travel by plane
- shopping for natural food and items that have not consumed too much energy in their transportation

- replacing household items only when necessary and not according to dictates of fashion
- recycling
- buying from charity shops
- using financial services that invest ethically
- not using shops that have exploitative employment practices
- avoiding excessive packaging

A year or so ago I heard a woman speak on the radio of having given up buying anything with plastic for Lent. It was not easy: she found, for instance, that she had to make her own yoghurt, because it was impossible to buy it without a plastic container. When I mentioned this to a neighbour in her late seventies, whom I would never have thought of as an activist, she said "For Lent? For ever!" She was one of those brave souls who strip the packaging off food that they have bought, and leave it in protest at the supermarket check-out.

The list above gives some opportunities for effecting change. It may seem irritating and time-consuming to spend so much time on such small daily activities. But the fact is that it is precisely in the smallest choices that we can make most change in the world – and in our own attitudes. And if we all do it, the effect on the planet will be palpable.

Once we begin to question our individual lifestyles, we become aware of the inequities of the wider system, and start to see the complexity of the choices. Do we stop buying bananas grown in a foreign land, or do we wish to support frail economies that are dependent on our consumption? Fair trade goods may still bring with them the carbon costs of their transport; organic food may not be fairly traded; the cocoa in our chocolate may have been grown under conditions of slavery.

We see how market forces depend on continuing growth, greater production and consumption, and greater waste. All of which put pressure on an already overburdened planet. It is not enough to wish for others what we have ourselves – it has been said that if all six billion people on the planet had a material standard of living like that of the UK, we would need three planets; for that of the USA, we would need seven. So, if the world is to be equitable, we have to be content with less.

When I gave up my car many years ago, it was for economic rather than green reasons. At first it seemed impossible: we were so reliant on the car to take the children to their activities. Some adjustments had to be made – we moved to a nearer nursery, a different piano teacher – and then a car-free existence became not only possible but pleasurable. For people living without adequate public transport, that may not be an option, but our choices are often wider than we at first realise.

The Lifestyle Movement is an organisation dedicated to these issues, working, it says, to provide inspiration and practical advice to people who aspire to live in a way that reflects the ideal of justice for the earth and for those who live on it. It combines a position on personal lifestyle with active support of groups working for environmental, developmental and peace issues. It seeks to inform its members on issues such as globalisation, international debt, resource use, genetically modified organisms, political exploitation and social justice and to point to the (often complex) connections between these issues.

The Slow Food movement, with over 100,000 members in 132 countries, aims to raise awareness about the sustainability of our food systems and social justice issues surrounding the food we eat. Involving both producers and consumers, they aim to bring systemic change to communities around the world.

From a religious standpoint, it is in our relationships with other people and the rest of the created world that God is expressed, so removing clutter that creates a barrier in that relationship is also a fundamental part of simplicity. The land must have its sabbaths too, we are told in Leviticus 25: there must be no exploitation. The reminder to care for the land that feeds us, to care for each other, redistributing land as needed, has ancient roots. It needs translating to modern circumstances, but the same principles still apply.

The issues that we have dealt with in this chapter may not feel in the least simple. It is easier to buy fast food, quicker to fly by jet, but in terms of global impact, the result will not be simplicity. The choices are complex, as is the process, but the result is one of simple justice and equality. The simplicity of leaving a light footprint on the earth is defined by not using up too many of earth's resources, for the sake of humankind and the earth.

Chapter 6

Worldliness

In so far as we are led towards true simplicity we will increasingly be called to dissent from a central thrust of the world we live in.
A statement from British Quakers, September 1997

The word "worldly" suggests adherence to material satisfactions. We live in a consumer-driven society, in which all of us – even students, patients and passengers – are considered "customers". Progress is marked by increases in material wealth. The push from advertising, the media, and our peers is towards bigger and more; the market thrives only by stirring us to a state of dissatisfaction. Success in the economy is defined only by growth. These attitudes are ingrained, copied by developing countries, and largely unquestioned until the recent world recession has driven many to reconsider these social concepts, some of which in their heart of hearts, perhaps, they have always felt to be false – and to reassess their life's priorities.

How did the definition of a nation's health become so tied to its economic state? Increasingly the measure of "wellbeing" in a wider qualitative, rather than quantitative, sense is establishing its place. As work by Richard Layard and others has revealed, an increase in material wealth does not lead to increased happiness. Examination of such wealthy nations as Japan, the United States and the UK shows that once our basic needs are met, an increase in wealth makes no difference to our level of happiness. This is not just anecdotally true, it is the story told by countless pieces of scientific research in such fields as psychology, neuroscience, economics, sociology and philosophy. Not only have we begun to question the concept of growth as our sole measure of success; increasingly it has become clear that continuing growth in all the world's economies is simply not sustainable. Populations grow, as does our use of the planet's all too finite resources. Continual global growth is not possible, and is damaging to the world.

In this context, we have begun to take a little more seriously the hugely radical move in the remote Kingdom of Bhutan to make the happiness of its people the measure of its success. The phrase "Gross National Happiness" was coined in the 1970s by its former king and has subsequently been developed into a sophisticated measure that not only represents a unifying vision for the country, but has been laid down as the foundation of its economic and development strategies.

If our purpose is to be true to our real selves, it is inevitable that we will at times find ourselves at odds with the prevailing mores. White lies, petty dishonesty, exaggeration of the truth – these are part of the everyday currency of the world we live in. As we become more sensitive to the movement of our inner lives, we may find our former complacency pinpricked into discomfort. Greed, lies, inequality – what have these to do with our real values? What is lacking in our own lives that we fill them with the ephemera of fashion or the vicarious excitement of celebrity gossip? As we listen to our inner promptings, our lives may move in a different direction, and we will feel out of synch with much that surrounds us. The tendency of our lives will have become counter-cultural.

It is hard to go against the stream, to make a conscious decision, for instance, to bring up children without giving in to the pressures of advertising, current trends and brand-names. It is hard not to be blinded by the status quo, not to be complicit in actions that we know in our hearts to be wrong. As religious and community leaders have found throughout the ages, making a stand for justice and equality is often unpopular, sometimes dangerous. We are born into a particular age, and have to learn to come to terms with it in the best way that we, as individuals with individual gifts, can, and set our priorities accordingly. We have to find a way of being true to our inner values while living in the world we have. Most of us find that we compromise in all sorts of ways until the discomfort becomes, once again, too great.

All major faiths have an ethical dimension: they are not just a set of beliefs but a way of living that expresses a set of values. The eight-fold path of Buddhism, for example, asks for not only Right belief, Right attention or collectedness and Right contemplation, but also Right will, Right speech, Right action, Right means of livelihood, and Right effort towards self-control. The chief obstructions to right living, it says, are the "three poisons" of greed, hatred, and delusion. Perhaps the most relevant to our discussion is greed, which is taken to include craving, attachment and envy: standard aspects of our daily life. "The values of faith", says Jonathan Dale, "are diametrically opposed to the values of the market...Love, truth, peace, community, equality point to an other-centredness wholly at odds with the market's relentless appeal to self" (59).

In living a life that is essentially counter-cultural, we will live at a critical distance from the values of those around us. If the manner of our lives is a witness to the centrality of love and justice, we will be taking a prophetic stance against what we see as the inequities of our age. "Dissent properly arises from clarity of vision, from seeing things as they really are. It is rooted in truth. And it reveals the truth. That was the role of the prophets of the Old Testament" (Dale, 28). And it takes courage, in the modern world no less than in the ancient, to express that dissent.

By questioning and rejecting some of the world's false practices we can also come to live with increased autonomy and less dependency on what we might have come to see as a dehumanising economy. We can move in a culture dominated

Chapter 7

Horse and cart

...these dark Satanic Mills
William Blake

Advocates of the simple life are divided in their opinion of technology. An extreme view is that the Industrial Revolution was the worst thing ever to happen to humankind. It is true that mechanisation deprived many of their employment and many traditional skills have been lost, some of them replaced by repetitive unskilled factory jobs. Mechanisation has increased our reliance on unrenewable energy sources but it has also led to huge advances in, for instance, medicine and in our knowledge and understanding of other cultures and the far reaches of the universe. It has saved many of us from back-breaking and time-consuming daily tasks. One result of the Industrial Revolution was a mass movement from the countryside to the cities, where most of us these days now live. Living a more simple life does not necessarily mean reverting to a more rural existence: simplicity has to be possible, here, in our world, where we are now.

Two religious communities known for their dedication to a simple life have widely differing attitudes to technology. The Shakers had no personal belongings, everything being communally owned, but in their daily lives they were not opposed to the use of, for instance, cars, telephones, and electricity. The Amish, on the other hand, though varying considerably in practice between local communities, do not in general use technology where it might interfere with their family life. Phones may be used outside the home; other technology may be used in their work.

In 2009 I spent a couple of months in a Ghanaian village without electricity. Contrary to my expectation, it was not the lack of light that troubled me – we went to bed early, and I had a wind-up lamp. But in extreme heat, the lack of a fan and a fridge made life difficult. With the exception of a few staples, food could not be stored and, with little fresh food available locally, people needed to walk about 4km to the nearest town to shop. Not surprisingly, fresh meat, fish and vegetables were often lacking from people's diets. (They were also too expensive.)

I now learn that electricity has been installed in the village, and wonder what that will mean for its inhabitants. While I was there, another British volunteer said that he thought electricity would be disastrous for the village, that noise levels (already high with loudspeakers charged by a few private generators) would increase, and people might be tempted to spend their limited resources on TV and music systems rather than on food, education and health care. I asked him then if he thought that electricity was disastrous for all of us. He pointed out that when we got electricity, none of the existing machines existed: we have had time to develop them slowly, and absorb them into our lives. People new to electricity are confronted with a whole battery of machines. TV advertising ensures that dissatisfaction is fed by a new sense of deprivation. I asked a local woman why she wanted electricity. She said, "So that my children can do their homework, and so that I don't fall in the dark when my torch fails." One cannot argue with that.

But at the opposite extreme that is our life in the West, houses, streets and transport are full of people wired up to their MP3 player, iPod or mobile phone or the now indispensable computer. In an increasingly virtual world, we are cutting ourselves off from each other's physical presence. As we walk down city streets, we have to dodge people whose eyes are cast down, unaware of their surroundings, attention devoted to messages on their mobile phones.

With our labour- and energy-saving devices, we are speeding up the pace of our lives. Saving our own very renewable physical energy to spend the earth's finite energy. What are we hurrying to, saving our labour for? Even the possibility of working at home, spending more time with the children, has led to an attitude in some towards "bleisure", a combination of business and leisure. While pushing our children on the swings in the park, we can be trawling through our emails on our mobile phones. Are we doing justice to either? Do the children feel our loving attention, our real presence?

We are also losing touch with the activities that machines have replaced. In a computer-filled world, handwriting is increasingly a thing of the past. How often do we receive, or write, a handwritten letter? So rarely, it seems, that the need to write long-hand for any length of time – as in an exam, for instance – taxes rarely used muscles. In a recent electricity cut following storms in the USA, one woman related how, as she could not use her electric clothes dryer, she had had to put her clothes on the bushes outside to dry – and, she said, "it worked"!

Choices

In Chapter 5 we looked at the impact our affluent lives in the West has on the rest of the world, and on our environment. Here we are considering what relation a more simple life might have to the technological advances of past centuries. Think about how many machines we use in an average day. When I get up, the central heating has already switched itself on, and water is heated as I run the tap. The fridge has been on all night. I switch on the light, the electric kettle to make a cup of tea, then I switch on my mobile phone, the computer and, later, the printer. I use a gas cooker, a vacuum cleaner, a radio, a land line, and a washing machine. Nearly everything I own: clothes, shoes, furniture, books, has been made by machine. Although, having given in to using a laptop, I am now a lapsed Luddite, I think of my life as pretty simple – I don't have a car, a microwave or a television – but it only takes something to go wrong for me to realise how reliant I am on power-guzzling machines.

Choices are never simple. We learn that using a dishwasher may actually use less water than washing dishes by hand – but we need also to consider the energy used to make the machine in the first place. Few people would want to give up the pleasure of hot water on tap, or to go back to washing our sheets by hand, but for many people moving to a simpler way of life does mean going back to some more traditional ways of doing things.

Concern about the use of pesticides, food preservatives and other additives, and GM, may lead people to avoid packaged food and use more fresh ingredients. Growing our own food has become increasingly popular in recession-hit times; even a small patch of ground can yield a surprising amount. Concern about the use of unrenewable energy sources may encourage us to avoid or reduce the use of our gadgets. Have we ever considered that toast is "twice-baked" bread?

But changing our behaviour in this way is not just about "concern" but an active pleasure: the delight of eating home-baked bread or home-made marmalade has not only to do with the superior quality of what we are eating but the pleasure of making it. The satisfaction of growing our own fruit and vegetables is undeniable and the taste unmatched by anything we can buy. A few seeds sown can be the beginning of a powerful process. Taking time, engaging ourselves in a mindful activity that uses our own hands and brings us close to the reality of the earth, is a joy in itself. Other such pleasures might include learning a traditional craft, such as drystone walling, beekeeping or thatching; learning a musical instrument, or taking up an old one. Making music with friends.

Finding time to include these kinds of activities may require a radical change of direction in our current lives; only small steps may be possible when we need to earn money to pay for our family's housing. But even small steps may show us the richness of taking time for pleasures that matter, and are likely to move us to further change. In this, as in everything else, simplicity is a life's journey.

Chapter 8

Joy

The world gives itself to us. It gives itself freely to us, if we can allow it. It showers us with gifts.
David Steindl-Rast

To live a simple life is to experience life more fully, to live with enhanced intensity and freedom. It is not a deprivation but a joy.

An enforced austerity, or actions taken for reasons of observance to some externally imposed rule, can lead to a distorted view of what simplicity means. An emphasis on sin, for instance, has led in some religions to extremes of self-abnegation, deprivation, even flagellation: a closed-in, obsessive attitude, lacking in generosity and with little regard to the needs of others. It can also lead to a mistaken concept of plainness. Among seventeenth-century North American Puritans, the pursuit of plainness for its own sake sometimes resulted in ugliness, meanness and mediocrity. Modern minimalism can be stark, hard, lacking the warmth of human connection.

Taken to excess, even simplicity in worship can take a wrong turning. The stripping away of ritual and holy objects from Protestant worship, in a reaction to what was seen as Popish excess, led early Quakers to consider the practice of the arts a distraction. Instead of their intention to assert the sanctity of all life, the exclusion of music and dance was a denial of the creative gifts of the Spirit, the joy at the heart of creation. Even the Trappist monk, Thomas Merton, was clear that simplicity did not involve the denial of beauty: its celebration, particularly in the natural world, is central to his writings.

Our response to the extreme consumerism of Western society

does not need to be equally extreme. Excess is as much a danger in the inner life as it is in the outer. Moderation, a balance between less and more, unmeasurable and personal in its definition, is at the heart of simplicity. The important thing is to be true to our own life's journey, open to the promptings of our own inner voice. There is no rule to adhere to; this is not a predictable path with a predetermined end. Allowing ourselves to be guided, letting go of goal-centred ambition, of the need to "arrive", will take us to unexpected places.

The simple life as described here is not a hair shirt. One of the blessings of owning less is that any addition feels like riches. In a large pot of expectation, a pint will feel little; in a half-pint measure, it will be full to overflowing. So, if we have a dozen pairs of shoes, another pair is not of much significance. If we own just one sari, another is luxury indeed. In seeking for more and more, we fail to understand this simple truth, this truth about simplicity. When I recently had an invasion of "stuff" held in storage to see if I would want it again, I found myself disabled by it, my mind as well as my physical space cluttered. Having done without it for nearly two years, I knew what I wanted, and that the rest could go. Shedding, once started, is a continuing activity, and the freedom is a delight.

This book does not advocate self-denial for its own sake, nor the prescription of a universal standard of material wealth. Pride in how little we have is just another expression of self-will. As discussed in Chapter 3, it is our attitude towards material objects and money that matters rather than the quantity. A large house can be used for hospitality. The generosity of open doors is an offering of the Spirit. Money is a tool; if shared with those who have less, or invested to humanely fruitful purpose, it is being used as a tool for good.

As one writer put it, "the effort should be to promote the participation of all in the abundance of the age rather than the extension of the privations of the past to all" (Quaker Quest, 6).

And what abundance there is! The created world is burgeoning with riches of all kinds: visual beauty, the joy of birdsong, the constantly changing seasons and landscape, vivid colour, the uniqueness of a leaf, a snowflake, the complex interactions of all created things. Simplicity includes taking less for granted, recapturing a relationship with everything around us.

And think of the mind and creativity of human beings. The art, music and language of peoples across the globe; the vast creativity and constantly growing understanding of scientists exploring every aspect of our world – from the instincts of fishes to the billions of galaxies that we can't even see. The complexity of the human brain is a marvel that we still do not understand.

A celebration of simplicity has nothing to do with life-denial. Living in the moment, with awareness of all that surrounds us, encourages us to reap joy from the small and the commonplace, as well as to wonder at the glories of creation and appreciate the complexities of our own gifts.

If we take a long look at what is really necessary in our lives, we will more easily find a balance in the reality of our material world. We will ensure that what we gain from scientific advances is not countered by a loss of connection with each other and with the rest of creation.

Chapter 9

The Emperor's new clothes

The Fool is purity of consciousness
Cecil Collins (4)

We all know of people described in the past as "a bit simple", people who may have mental health problems or learning difficulties, who are perceived as having "something lacking". But, as times move on, there is increased understanding of difference, difference that can hide exceptional perceptions. My father was a schizophrenic, and a deeply spiritual man. Although it was always clear that he understood much that the rest of us did not, it was only after his death that I realised how much his life had to teach me. Chris Goodchild is autistic and has written with great emotional openness of what that can mean: "Autism is a blessing, a gifted way of seeing the world. It is also deeply misunderstood" (17). How hard it is to live with difference of this kind is expressed in the title of his book, *A Painful Gift*.

In the tradition of the jester, the clown and the fool there is some recognition that conventional behaviour does not reveal the whole truth. Wise monarchs kept a jester at their side to pierce the falseness of their courtiers' subservient posturing. Whether such a role was innate or donned for the purpose, the clown or fool in Shakespeare's plays is often the channel for wisdom, a simple naïvety cutting through the nonsense of received wisdom in the circles of power.

Holy fools
Every culture has its traditions and folktales about fools. In most

religious traditions, the concept of "holy fool" is an important one, particularly in Sufism and Zen. As Cecil Collins relates, fools represent "the eternal virginity of spirit, which in the dark winter of the world, continually proclaims the existence of new life, giving faithful promise of the spring of an invisible kingdom, and the coming of light" (10).

In Christianity, St Francis of Assisi was famously described by G.K. Chesterton as "God's Tumbler"; Jesus himself has been called the Divine Fool, his life and teachings a subversion of conventional society, opening himself up to ridicule, persecution and, finally, crucifixion. In the Jewish scriptures, the Talmud refers to jesters as bringing redemption, and in Islam, the figure of Nasreddin is legendary. Possibly a real imam in the thirteenth century, he became a folk hero, his "foolish" behaviour pointing to the hidden truth. An earlier Sufi, Abu Sa'id, also figures widely. "In the eleventh century, the *majzub* [Sufi holy fool] Abu Sa'id was the focus of constant gossip because of his erratic and 'irreligious' behaviour." (See http://www.thenoodlebowl.com /jesters/)

Collins considers that the concept of "Fool" has a wider application, including priests, artists, anyone who opens themselves up to the spontaneity and innocence of creative life. Indeed, it extends beyond the particularity of individuals.

> I believe that there is in life, and in the human psyche, a certain quality, an inviolate eternal innocence, and this quality I call the fool. It is a continuous wisdom and compassion that heals with fun and magic. It is the joy in the original Adam in men (7).

A few years ago I took a course of clowning evening classes which showed me a lighter way of being. The concepts of innocence, play, and above all a trusting goal-lessness, were instrumental in a simple way of working that allowed the natural course of events to occur rather than pushing to make things happen.

Alan Watts expresses it well: "This is not a philosophy of not looking where one is going; it is a philosophy of not making where one is going so much more important than where one is, that there will be no point in going" (145).

The Emperor's new clothes

The fable of the Emperor's new clothes illustrates the point. An emperor defined only by his vanity hires two weavers who promise to make him the most beautiful suit from a fabric invisible to anyone who was unfit for his position or "just hopelessly stupid". For fear of appearing unfit for his position or stupid, the Emperor pretends that he can see the cloth; his ministers do the same. When he parades in front of his people, all behave as if he is gloriously clothed. It is not until a child calls out: "The Emperor's got no clothes on" that the pretence is dissolved.

Christ rebuked his disciples for preventing children from coming to him to be blessed, an event that significantly occurs in three of the gospels. Indeed, he called for us to become as little children: "Verily, I say unto you, Whosoever shall not receive the kingdom of God as a little child, he shall not enter therein" (Mark 10:15 AV).

Living with children can bring us a little understanding of what is meant. If we allow ourselves to be open to the freshness of their perceptions, children can help us learn the world anew, seeing its glory through the eyes of innocence. Our learnt cynicism is negative, deadening, and shuts our eyes to the beauty of the world, the wonder of creation and our part in it.

But what does it mean for us to become as a little child? If we are not gifted with an enduring innocence, the kind of mind that stays childlike, we have to work to recapture that sensibility, to learn an innocence based on our experience of life. And this is hard work. "Only the most highly disciplined artist", says Aldous Huxley, "can recapture, on a higher level, the spontaneity of the child with its first paint-box" (134). Perhaps one of the drives towards simplicity is to find adventure in the everyday, to be closer to the adventure of living, and look for what in Zen is called the Essential world in all of this.

Buddhists talk of "a beginner's mind": an attitude of innocence, naïvety, a childlike openness. According to the Zen teacher, Shunryu Suzuki:

We have to remain always beginner's mind. This is the secret of Zen, and secret of various practices – practice of flower arrangement, practice of Japanese singing, and various art...So, if you can keep your beginner's mind forever, you are Buddha. In this point, our practice should be constant. We should practice our way with beginner's mind always. There is no need to have deep understanding about Zen. Even though you read Zen literature you have to keep this beginner's mind. You have to read it with fresh mind.

1965 Zen Mind, Beginner's Mind lecture

Chapter 10

Letting go

A condition of complete simplicity
(Costing not less than everything)
T.S. Eliot, "Little Gidding" in *Four Quartets*

It is not just in order to share the poverty of others that we might be drawn to a simpler way of life. It might be in recognition that simpler ways of life practised by people without much choice are actually better, and that most of what we possess we could happily do without. The phrase "less is more" may seem like a modern cliché. In fact it has been around for hundreds of years, first encapsulated in print by the poet Robert Browning. A friend of mine said she had been thinking about what she needed to survive, and came up with the following list: "clean water, enough food, medicines for when I am sick, a roof over my head, some basic clothing, some paper and a pencil – and", she said, "I do like my TV." Our own lists might be very different, and rather longer, but when we come to think of it, what we actually need is surprisingly little.

As discussed in Chapter 8, a simple way of life is no kind of mortification or deprivation. Whether in worship or daily life, external simplicity is an outer expression of an inner freedom, a detachment. Simplicity in outer things allows us to order our inner life, and, as we become more attuned to our inner life, a simplification of externals, less "clutter", may become not a duty nor an expression of social or political views, but a mystic necessity. As we described in Chapter 2, when the discomfort becomes too great, we can do no other. And there's no going back: discarding, it seems, is progressive; moving towards freedom is addictive, and we may well find what we have discarded distasteful.

We are not, however, just talking of an external process. In Chapter 3 we looked at developing a less attached attitude to our material belongings. But non-attachment goes deeper. Letting go of ambition, attachment to the fruits of labour – success or failure; letting go of the need to please, to be loved, to be in control – belongings of another kind, these are harder lessons to learn. Clearing out these attachments is part of the journey to the riches of simplicity. Only when we let go of our own willing, only when we accept what is given to us in life, and allow ourselves to be guided, will there be an opening for the inflowing of grace and transformation.

"'Our kingdom go'", says Aldous Huxley, "is the necessary and unavoidable corollary of 'Thy kingdom come'" (113). What does this mean? It means that while we are full of self-regard, self-importance, self-will, there will be no room for the Spirit; there will be too much ego-noise for the still small voice to be heard. St John of the Cross wrote, "The goods of God, which are beyond all measure, can only be contained in an empty and solitary heart" (in *ibid.*, 123).

Working at developing that emptiness, of letting go of the demands of the swollen ego, is a lifetime's work.

Our desire to be simple, to serve the one God, is always only that: a desire, an intention. It is never finished but always in process. That process is also the process of self-knowledge: the confrontation between the deepest Self which is the Image of God in us, and the more superficial layers: the levels of ego that interacts with the world, that attaches and puts security in objects which are less than ultimate, that puts on faces or masks to try to please or win the esteem of others. There lies within us, as a perpetual call, the possibility of reaching that place of simple being without pretence or affectation, where the interior is directly reflected outwardly with no obstruction or deflection or deviation.

Prevallet, 14-15

Even if we no longer cling to material possessions, we do not so lightly let go of our need for security, our internal clinging. When I was led in my fifties to let go of my old career *without any need to know* what would follow, I finally understood how it was to live in the way of trust, guidance, and faith. Letting go in the inner life, as in material things, brings an extraordinary freedom.

> Give over thine own willing, give over thy own running, give over thine own desiring to know or be anything, and sink down to the seed which God sows in thy heart and let that grow in thee and be in thee and breathe in thee and act in thee; and thou shalt find by sweet experience that the Lord knows that and loves and owns that, and will lead it to the inheritance of Life, which is its portion.
>
> Isaac Penington, 1661

At core, we are embracing our true selves, and manifesting that in the way we live our lives. The simplification of our life becomes "an inner condition made visible". The simplicity of Shaker furniture is an expression of the truth of its makers. It was in giving their deepest attention to the task that they were able to create something that most simply fitted its purpose.

The Religious Society of Friends (Quakers) does not have a creed, but adheres to testimonies that encompass a way of life. One of the four usually cited is to "simplicity", which began as a reaction to the extravagance and snobbery of seventeenth-century England and has continued to be interpreted according to contemporary circumstance. While all testimonies are open to individual understanding, simplicity has always been seen by

Quakers as a return to the truth. The American Quaker, Rufus Jones, felt that "unclouded honesty at the heart and centre of a man is the true basis of simplicity".

It is asking a lot. We have many roles in life: parent, child, client, patient, lover – and we take on many more in our working lives, some of which have established an identity which gives us status, something with which we are comfortable. Do we always speak with our authentic voice, from an undivided heart? Or do we allow our role of the moment to express a partial truth? Do we freely open ourselves up to God, or are there secret reservations? All of us live with compromise.

At the heart of simplicity is an interaction between our inner self and our outward actions: a constantly changing balance. Outer distraction or distortion reflects an inner fragmentation. But it is not a one-way process. We have probably all had the experience of clearing our desk or worktable, and finding that the external order clears our mind. Spiritually speaking, as we feel moved to simplify our life, in whatever way, the increase in clarity and freedom will allow space for growth in our spiritual journey. It is an ongoing and reciprocal process. The more our outward actions stem from the essence of our being, the less will stand in the way of a calm and authentic life, the less clutter there will be between us and Reality.

"We are rich when we know what is important, and where our hearts are" (Quaker Quest, 21). What we are talking about is a focus on the essential, the essence, the Spirit, in every part of our lives. As we look for the essence in other things and people, so we ourselves will be refined: our own essence shines through and we are able to act from that place. We will be in a place of integrity (literally "wholeness").

In the Judeo-Christian tradition, the whole notion of simplicity may be seen as stemming from the simplicity of the Divine Itself.

In Christian thought, God as a simple being is not divisible; God is simple, not composite, not made up of thing upon thing. In other words, the characteristics of God are not parts of God that together make God what he is. Because God is simple, his properties are identical with himself, and therefore God does not *have goodness*, but simply *is goodness*.

> Wikipedia

And in Judaism:

God's existence is absolutely simple, without combinations or additions of any kind. All perfections are found in Him in a perfectly simple manner. However, God does not entail separate domains – even though in truth there exist in God qualities which, within us, are separate...Indeed the true nature of His essence is that it is a single attribute, (yet) one that intrinsically encompasses everything that could be considered perfection. All perfection therefore exists in God, not as something added on to His existence, but as an integral part of His intrinsic identity.

> Moshe Chaim Luzzatto, Derekh Hashem I:1:5

But do we respond with the unequivocal simplicity that is called for? If we have been created in the image of God, then we too, with God's help, have the potential for that simplicity. The simplicity of God, of truth, of love. In a life devoted to God's purpose, the stripping down of the inessentials pares away the context of life: one is more purely an instrument of purpose. As Thomas Kelly writes, "The simplified man loves God with all his heart and mind and soul and strength and abides trustingly in that strength" (75). Reducing the clutter in our lives, whether in material objects, use of time or money, or in our religious practices, leads to an increased clarity of vision and a focus; a view of life and its priorities that is in itself simple. We can move

Further reading

Collins, Cecil, *The Vision of the Fool*. Chipping Norton: Anthony Kedros, new edition 1981

Dale, Jonathan (ed.), *Faith in Action*. London: Quaker Home Service, 2000

Elgin, Duane, *Voluntary Simplicity*. New York: Morrow, 1998

Goodchild, Christopher, *A Painful Gift*. London: Darton, Longman and Todd, 2009

Hanh, Thich Nhat, *Present Moment, Wonderful Moment*. Berkeley, Ca.: Parallax Press, 1990

Huxley, Aldous, *The Perennial Philosophy*. London: Chatto & Windus, 1946

Kelly, Thomas, *A Testament to Devotion*. New York: first publication, Harper & Brothers, 1941; new edition, HarperCollins, 1992

Lane, John, *Timeless Simplicity*. Totnes, Devon: Green Books, 2001

Layard, Richard, *Happiness: Lessons from a New Science*. London: Penguin, 2006

Prevallet, Elaine M., *Reflections on Simplicity*. Pendle Hill Publications, first edition 1982, reprint 2000

Quaker Quest, *Twelve Quakers and Simplicity*. London: Quaker Quest, 2006

Suzuki, D.T., *An Introduction to Zen Buddhism*. London: Rider reissue, 1991

Taber, Frances Irene, *Finding the Taproot of Simplicity*. Pendle Hill Publications, 2009

Watts, Alan W., *The Way of Zen*. London: Penguin, reprint 1970

www.enoughisplenty.net

www.thenoodlebowl.com/jesters/

www.slowfood.org.uk

BOOKS

O is a symbol of the world, of oneness and unity. In different cultures it also means the "eye," symbolizing knowledge and insight. We aim to publish books that are accessible, constructive and that challenge accepted opinion, both that of academia and the "moral majority."

Our books are available in all good English language bookstores worldwide. If you don't see the book on the shelves ask the bookstore to order it for you, quoting the ISBN number and title. Alternatively you can order online (all major online retail sites carry our titles) or contact the distributor in the relevant country, listed on the copyright page.

See our website **www.o-books.net** for a full list of over 500 titles, growing by 100 a year.

And tune in to myspiritradio.com for our book review radio show, hosted by June-Elleni Laine, where you can listen to the authors discussing their books.

mySpiritRadio